Shoe Leather

PRACTICE FOSTERING THE HARVEST

RICK OGLESBY

"Now, put that into shoe leather" is a phrase often heard in the South. It means to walk out (shoes on the ground) what you have learned. This material helps you put "shoe leather" to *Fostering The Harvest*, a workshop on evangelism produced by Biblical Ministries Worldwide.

The *Fostering The Harvest* DVD contains the *Shoe Leather* lectures and question-and-answer sessions with local church members who desired to implement *Fostering The Harvest* throughout their church. Thus, this workbook is a companion to the *Fostering The Harvest* material. Use this as a teaching aid or a follow-up workshop for those in your church who will take *Fostering The Harvest* to the next level.

Grace to you as you put "shoe leather" into your ministry to reach the lost for Jesus Christ.

Shoe Leather

To order more copies of this book, contact Amazon at 866.216.1072 or at www.amazon.com.

All Scripture quotations, unless otherwise indicated, are taken from The English Standard Version. Copyright © 2001 by Crossway Bibles, Wheaton, IL. All rights reserved.

ISBN 978-1475089387

Printed in the United States of America

Return the Cross to Golgotha

By George MacLeod

I simply argue that the cross be raised again
At the center of the market place
As well as on the steeple of the church.

I reassert the truth that
Jesus was not crucified in a sanctuary
Between two candles,

But on a cross between two thieves,
In a town garbage heap;
At a crossroad of politics so cosmopolitan
That they had to write His title
In Hebrew and in Latin and in Greek...

And at the kind of place
Where cynics talk smut
And thieves curse and soldiers gamble.

That is where He died
And that is what He died about.
And that is where Christ's followers are to be,
And what His people are to be about.

Table of Contents

Sessions

PRACTICE FOSTERING THE HARVEST

Help To Recognize An Evangelist

Is there someone in your church whom you think might be an evangelist? Do you wonder if you may be one? Here's a simple way to evaluate a person's affinity for evangelism. Check each box that UNDOUBTEDLY describes them. Choose quickly. The person

- ☐ 1. Consistently talks about witnessing to others
- ☐ 2. Enjoys helping others in the community
- ☐ 3. Finds it easy to meet and speak with others
- ☐ 4. Accepts calculated risks
- ☐ 5. Knows his neighbors
- ☐ 6. Learns by doing
- ☐ 7. Can fail without lasting loss of confidence
- ☐ 8. Treats work/neighborhood as a mission field
- ☐ 9. Has an interest in the church doing some community service
- ☐ 10. Regularly requests prayer for lost persons
- ☐ 11. Tries new things and adapts to change fairly easily
- ☐ 12. Needs a little help in organization
- ☐ 13. Has unsaved friends with whom he/she does things
- ☐ 14. Encourages others in evangelism, relating, etc.
- ☐ 15. Often "shadows" the pastor and peppers him with questions
- ☐ 16. Prefers ministry outside the church rather than in church programs
- ☐ 17. Sometimes gets frustrated with church meetings or internal focus
- ☐ 18. Reads secular materials
- ☐ 19. Teaches or is willing to learn to teach
- ☐ 20. Is proactive in greeting visitors

In my experience, the following traits have *always* marked those whom I consider an evangelist in the churches that I led: 1, 3, 5, 7, 8, 9, 10, 11, 13, 14, 16, 19, 20. These are just my opinions, so be sure to think through the observations carefully.

Once you have identified an evangelist, enable him/her to carve out a working relationship with the pastor to mentor the evangelist in theology and ministry; help him/her to reach out, train, and motivate others to reach out and to encourage outreach.

Many believers want to build relational bridges with unbelievers but are a little stymied about getting started. We may find it hard to think of what to say to a new acquaintance, or we may feel pressured to do things the right way.

A couple of things can help us. First, there are some simple steps for getting started that anyone can learn. My wife and I trained our children to use these skills when they were five years old. They are all parents now and continue to use them. Train church members in them, and they will be more comfortable and effective when greeting church guests.

Another helpful reminder is to not think about doing it "right." Right and wrong carry moral overtones and can make us feel guilty or as if we've failed, both of which kill motivation. Instead, just tell yourself that you are learning to meet people well. Take it out of the pass-fail arena and develop a skill-learning mindset.

How To Form A Conversation

Everyone enjoys talking about him or herself; we all want to be the focus of someone's interest to one degree or another. Not everyone is readily open or responsive, but we all build life around a FORM comprised of common life connections. You can get to know a lot about a person quickly if you FORM them with some simple, open-ended questions.

Imagine that you are at your first Chamber of Commerce meeting. You are there to make both business and eternal connections, but you don't yet know anyone. You decide to introduce yourself to the guy at the snack table. As you exchange names and handshakes, you start to FORM him. You ask him about one of these four areas and follow where the conversation leads:

- **Family:** Tell me about your family. How old are your kids? Are you married? How long? How'd you two meet? Where are your parents? Is that your hometown?

- **Occupation:** What do you do? How'd you get into that? How long have you done that? What's your greatest job challenge? How does social media affect your industry? Where did you go to college? How did it prepare you for your job?

- **Recreation:** What's your favorite sport? How'd you get into it? Who is your favorite team? When's the last time that you saw them play? What sports do your kids play?

- **Money:** How do feel about the current stock market situation? What do you think we ought to do about national debt? What's a good book you've read on finances? What do you think the economy holds for our kids when they're adults? Where do you want to live when you retire? Tell me about it.

As you can see, these questions easily open the door to shared life connections. As you listen and question the other person, you make him feel important and interesting – and that can prompt him to like you, often the first step in the privilege of sharing life in Christ.

How To Build On New Relationships With Lost Persons

Becoming familiar with someone via FORM often opens doors for future interaction. You want to "redeem the time" and be proactive with your newly made connection. When you do this, you will set yourself apart as an above average believer.

According to the Barna Research Group, after the average believer has followed Jesus for two years, he/she has NO relationships with lost persons. He/she knows many but fails to connect with them in any meaningful way. This should not be.

Speaking with His Father, Jesus said, "*As you sent me into the world, so I have sent them into the world.*" Now, why did the Father send Jesus? "*To seek and to save that which was lost.*" Why then did Jesus send us? "*To seek and to save that which was lost.*"

The world into which our Lord sends us is drastically different than our norms. America's worldview is no longer theistic, morally Christian, or accepting of Christ followers. Where once we could present the gospel assuming that we'd be understood, we can no longer do so. We hold presuppositions that most persons do not. Many unsaved picture Christianity with the colors of television evangelists, YouTube videos, and broadcast caricatures like Ned on the Simpsons.

Christianity, as our culture sees it is a philosophy that's been tried and found wanting. It is old news, not good news. It is a cramp on a lifestyle rather than a freeing gift. How do we infiltrate such mindsets so that people understand the sweet grace of Christ's gospel? Two absolutes must be accepted and applied. First, relational evangelism is the best method now. People want to be loved and accepted, and that gives us a great foundation for connecting to communicate. Second, teaching to communicate the gospel within that relationship must usually replace simply sharing the facts of the gospel and a call to respond. Those facts are just not recognized or accepted as in the past.

How do we connect with unbelievers after meeting them so that we can communicate Christ to them? Chapters 1 and 2 of John reveal several insights into how Jesus made eternal connections with his first disciples and other lost people. We can transfer these practices to our culture and harness His tactics for building redemptive relationships.

Explore Their Spiritual Interests (1:35-39)

These two unnamed disciples of John shared spiritual interests. John the Baptist pointed them to Jesus who further questioned them: He asked WHAT do you seek, not WHOM do you seek. He built on their spiritual concerns.

Good news! All people have spiritual interests. They're not always interested in Christ; they may even be anti-Christianity. But don't be afraid to discuss their religion nor hesitate to ask them to explain their beliefs to you. God created us with spiritual interests; all people have them, and fishers of men can tap them. Remember, ask, listen, and DO NOT attempt to correct. Get to know their religious worldview.

Be Question Oriented (1:35-38)

The first thing that Jesus did was to ask an open-ended question (1:38). This unlocked the door for them to reveal their expectations of the one whom John proclaimed. It's more important in the early stages of connecting with the lost to ask than to answer. Listen for their worldview, interests, needs, hurts, life expectations, and religious beliefs. Try to pick up their passions. As you do, you will learn "eternal contact" points.

Be Hospitable (1:39)

Jesus' next words were an invitation to His place. It was 10 in the morning, and they spent that day with him. Be hospitable. Use your home, boat, round of golf, or grill to get together with the unsaved. Sitting around your living room, sharing a Coke, or standing around your smoking grill can go a long way toward eternity. Be welcoming and sharing.

Build On Family Ties (1:40-42)

Andrew brought his brother Peter to Jesus who then reached him. You will get to know the family members of your lost friends. These are often good foundations for outreach. Build on them! Cookouts, sporting events, birthday parties – all are good relationship builders.

Network Business Relationships (1:43-51)

Andrew, Peter, and Philip shared a common occupation - fishing. The Lord harnessed their business network to extend His saving work. Capture the relationships you have in the business world and develop them for Christ. Be active in Kiwanis, Rotary, Chamber of Commerce, or your home builders association. Great opportunity is often disguised as a business contact.

Be Affirming (1:42, 47)

Jesus recognized and affirmed the characters of Peter and Nathanael. What a wonderful insight into our King's personality: he looks for the good in persons and notes it when he finds it. How often do you receive positive feedback at work? It seems that most communication at work is corrective. How refreshing to be an affirming person. Honest, specific recognition of a person's strengths and positive traits is valuable.

Share Social Events (2:1-11)

Jesus and His men accepted the invitation to a wedding where people partied and celebrated one of life's greatest pleasures for seven days. You too should join in the social celebrations and events of the lost. Host Super Bowl parties at your house, and invite lost friends. Go to the office Christmas party and be a designated driver if needed. Social events are great for redemptive relating.

Be A Servant (2:1-11)

We all know that Jesus turned water into the best wine ever tasted. But we sometimes forget that he showed that part of his glory (11) is to be a servant. Let's proactively meet people's needs. Loan your neighbor a tool. Cut their grass. Keep their dog when they go on vacation.

I have a lost friend who regularly comes to see me because I helped him with some plumbing issues. In fact, he recently walked to my house with an injured leg just to give me a CD and talk. Let's keep serving others outside the family of God.

To sum up, **harness everyday life** to make contact with lost persons. These tactics put lost folks at ease, for they occur on neutral turf rather than a church building. List your lost acquaintances. Thank God for each, and start praying for your involvement in their lives. Brainstorm on ways to connect.

Imagine the pleasure you will feel knowing that you're pleasing Christ. Envision the opportunities you will enjoy. Anticipate the growth that you will experience through new relationships and the sense of eternal activity in your fellowship. GO FISH!

As previously mentioned, you need to grasp how the lost in your community see life and what some of their felt needs are. Many of our churches recoil from the term, *felt needs*. Actually, we all came to Christ because of felt needs – everyone does. We all go to church, serve the Lord, and relate to others because of felt needs. Jesus certainly met felt needs: leprosy, blindness, demonism, fear of drowning, hunger, need for acceptance, etc. The issue with using felt needs to reach people is how we ultimately present the gospel.

A felt-need oriented ministry replaces the gospel of release from sin and condemnation with a gospel of need meeting and life improvement. Does Christ improve our lives? Absolutely! But is an improved life the good news? Absolutely not! However, felt needs are an avenue to get to the heart of the issue. We must be aware of and responsive to some of them as we grasp how lost persons see life.

We Must Work To Grasp Our Community

The longer that you are a Christian the more you see life through a church sub-culture grid. Try this: record how you think versus your lost friends:

	BELIEVER	UNSAVED
SUNDAY		
SEX		
ETHICS		

There are some major differences aren't there? We think differently, and we speak in a different way than out lost friends. We have developed our own language (Christianese) that the unchurched do not understand: PTL, VBS, sanctuary, the Word, sanctification, salvation, the blood, etc.

I once told a man about a wonderful thing that God did. I was president of a Bible college, and we had prayed and worked hard to achieve a God-sized strategic plan, and He graciously did it. My friend listened intently then said, "Why do you say praise the Lord for what He did? Didn't you do all the work?" We must work to grasp their thinking.

Two ways to get to know your community and its people are demographic and ethnographic research.

Demographic Research

Meaning: Polls, surveys and statistics that describe your locale. Demographics statistically describe the number of families/households/ income data/races within a specific distance or drive time of your church building. Demographics are helpful but they are usually interpreted by those removed from the community. They provide little or no personal or worldview information.

Methods: Search the Net, and speak with your local Chamber of Commerce. Use these:
- http://factfinder2.census.gov/faces/nav/jsf/pages/index.xhtml
- http://www.lifeway.com/menu/200902/
- http://city-data.com
- http://map.nazarene.org
- http://www.perceptgroup.com/

Ethnographic Research

Meaning: Your community's worldviews and makeup, insights into the people of your area. Ethnographics includes these types of elements:

- Likes & dislikes: food preferences, sports teams, neighborhood pride, etc.
- Social Structures: families, schools, parks, churches, blue collar/white collar, education
- World Views: generational poverty; Millennials, etc.
- Religious Heartbeats: denominations, pagan, theistic, secular

Methods: Our goal is to understand the people in our community. We use

- Observations: Examine as you drive by, shop, buy gas, work, etc.
- Questions: What do you think about . . . ? What's your take on . . . ? Listen!
- Relationships: neighborhood BBQ's, a gym buddy, PTA, soccer coach
- Conversations: At work, school, gym, golf course, mall
- Incarnation: Do what you like to do with the unchurched where they do it.

This method seeks to understand your community via relationships. It is slow, but when the church body pursues it, it is VERY effective for realizing community opportunities and needs to develop an evangelistic strategy. You will be most effective reaching those whose culture you share and understand.

A Biblical Example of Ethnographic Research (Acts 17:16-34)

Paul's experience in Athens illustrates both the use of ethnographic research and how to harness it for the gospel's sake.

Paul Observed
- Their varied worldviews and mores (17-21)
- Their primary connections to hearing of Christ (18-21; 16; 22-23)
- Their secular materials (28)

Paul Felt
- Emotionally disturbed at the idolatry (16)
- Gospel driven rather than indifferent to the darkness (17)

Paul Responded
- Dialogued, proclaimed, and taught the truth (17-31)
- Expected and accepted opposition (18, 32)
- Commended rather than criticized (22-23)
- Made Christ, not culture or behaviors, the issue (18-20)
- Focused on belief rather than behaviors (27, 34)

Don't assume that you are aware of how the lost subculture thinks. They have their own worldview just like we believers do. Make the time to determine how to get your congregation involved in doing ethnographic research. Perhaps have a meal after church and ask them what they see. Record these observations and you are on your way!

One of the most natural and effective places to share the good news, from the life of Jesus until now, has been the home. In an increasingly non-Christian society, the Jesus follower will become friends with and evangelize people where his Lord did—in the home and in the marketplace. Jesus and Paul both used home studies often.

The Evangelistic Bible Study Goal

Our goal is to teach the unsaved, win them to Christ, start them toward healthy discipleship, and fully integrate them into the life of church. Our confidence is in the Lord, His Word and prayer, not the method. This is simply one way to help lost people hear His Word.

The Evangelistic Bible Study Benefits

- It occurs on neutral territory that is comfortable to the unsaved.
- It encourages dialogue, which is necessary for changing a worldview.
- It communicates the love of God practically.
- It communicates the Gospel clearly, simply, comprehensively, and naturally.
- People are saved, and they come to faith partially grounded.
- New believers accept Scripture as their authority.
- It naturally and powerfully makes evangelism a team ministry.

The Evangelistic Bible Study Team

A successful evangelistic Bible study is a team activity. Team members include a host or hostess, a teacher, one Christian single or couple, and several others who will join the team in prayer but not attend the study. It is critical that few believers be present as they tend to innocently and unknowingly control the discussions.

The most significant person in an evangelistic Bible study may be the **host** or **hostess**. They usually create the atmosphere. They are the driving force behind the study and the ones primarily responsible for getting others involved. An effective host has

- The ability to make people feel at home and secure
- Healthy relationships with lost people
- The ability to learn and use the names of attendees
- The ability to listen and start a conversation
- A sensitivity to peoples felt needs: temperature, ventilation, lighting
- Clarity on the purpose of the study
- An ability to focus on belief rather than behavior

The **teacher** is also significant. He/she must be simple, clear, relational, very illustrative, and non-defensive. He/she must be able to encourage questions and interaction and not stand on his soapbox. The evangelistic Bible study teacher must also respect the belief systems of others (remember Paul in Athens?). He/she will use these beliefs to create a bridge to the lost person's heart. The teacher will never make fun of or reject the beliefs of the unsaved, but rather use them as avenues for study. For instance, when challenged about evolution, he might say something like, *"Well I'm not an evolutionist but I understand the position. I am a creationist. And this is very interesting because both are faith systems. Why don't we talk about the object of our faith?"*

Effective evangelistic Bible studies build around personal, felt needs. All men want a return on their investments, so study subjects that interest them. It's always a great idea to survey your lost friends and see what they would like to study. Some examples that lost people have asked to study include

- The family
- Husband-wife submission
- Creation and evolution
- Why Christians are so judgmental
- Child raising
- How the Bible fits together
- Why is there so much evil in the world?
- The Gospel of John
- What does the Bible say about the future?
- What is the Rapture?
- Why are there so many denominations?

You can easily see how these can whet the appetite of a lost person if properly done.

Team members must remember never to press an unsaved person for a decision and never to rush them to trust Christ. In the book of Acts, you discover that lost persons always ask the believers what they should do to be saved. The preachers of Acts never pressed nor did they give up at the first sign of resistance. When the Holy Spirit is drawing a lost person to the Lord Jesus Christ, he/she will want to know what to do.

What about **Christians** at the study? They should always be in a minority role. The studies are aimed at the lost, and all believers present should serve in a supportive role. They are there to help provide a relaxed atmosphere, initiate conversation and help the host or hostess. Christians should only rarely answer questions and should be warned to keep their opinions and "informed" questions to themselves. Remember, this is not for the growth of believers but to reach the lost. Christian attendees must avoid such things as

- Religious clichés or terminology such as born again, saved, sanctification, etc.
- Criticism of other groups or denominations
- Correcting doctrinal errors or wrong answers
- Going to cross references

- An easily understandable Bible in the same edition for each person
- A handout or whiteboard or both
- The Holy Spirit: He brings clarity and conviction to the lost, and He empowers you
- Prayer: you and others will see God answer

Lay A Foundation for the Evangelistic Bible Study

Evangelistic Bible studies come in all shapes and sizes. I've done them from one on one all the way to a group of three believers and twenty-four lost persons. Smaller studies are probably with friends who already know you. But if you involve many folks, some of whom don't know one another or the believers involved, here are some suggestions:

- Pray, asking God for specific people to invite
  - Make a list of names
  - Pray consistently for the people on your list
  - Expect results
  - Pray over your team

- Set a specific date and location
  - Give at least four weeks lead time
  - Avoid holidays

- Send or speak effective invitations
  - Maybe have a coffee, potluck dinner, or lunch for people to meet.
  - Invite your friends in writing to that event.
  - At the event, let your friends know a future Bible study is the main intention.
  - For coffee, lunch, or dinner, invite two times the number you can handle.
  - Follow up with a phone call two to three days before the meeting. You have not because you phone not.
  - Never worry about the number who come - Jesus speaks to all size groups.
  - Expect cancellations from one half to two hours before the meeting -- don't be disappointed by these.

- Tell them that for the first study you would like to do an overview of the Bible and how it fits together - just to give everyone greater comfort. Ask if that would satisfy them. If acceptable, plan to do so.
- With group input, establish the date, time, and place. With group input, determine what to do about children.
- Send a written invitation before the study. Follow it up with a phone call two to three days prior to the study.

- The study should meet every week for at least 4 weeks, but let your context determine this. Take breaks for certain times of the year: Christmas and New Year, Spring break, summer vacation, etc.

How to Conduct an Evangelistic Bible Study

- Things to Do
  - Have participants bring refreshments. They like to share the fun.
  - Make people comfortable.
  - Talk about things people are interested in before the study.
  - Turn off the phone.
  - The study team must mix with the lost people.
  - Be sensitive to timid or turned-off people.
  - Limit your Bible study to 45 or 60 minutes maximum. Start and finish on time.
  - Encourage questions and interaction.
  - Cover all material planned, even if you summarize.
  - Love people; don't force anything on them.

- Things to Not Do
  - Play Christian music or use Christian lingo.
  - Talk about your church, berate or even discuss other religious groups.
  - Talk with the other Christians.

Preparing the Study

- Pray, asking the Spirit to teach and lead you.
- Read through the passage several times.
- Prepare a handout with questions based on the passage, or have a white board.

Teaching the Study

Materials and Involvement

- Pass out the same edition Bibles as needed.
- Give the page number.
- Give handouts with questions.
- Let people work in groups of 2-3 if possible.
- Introduce the topic. Give necessary background information on the passage.
- Give them time to examine the questions and the passage. Encourage discussion.
- Elicit their feedback. Use different techniques: drama, role-play, buzz groups.
- Stay in one chapter - don't skip around the Bible.
- Use a white board or large pad to record people's insights.
- Know your purpose and stick to it; don't go off on rabbit trails.

Questions that Stimulate Discussion
- What does the verse/passage tell us about Jesus?
- What does the verse/passage tell us about us?
- What does the verse/passage tell us about the main characters?
- How do you think you could apply this passage?
- Can any of you identify with this person?
- Have you had any experience similar to this?

Handling Wrong Answers to Questions
- Don't embarrass the person by saying, "No, that's incorrect." If any part of the answer is right, mention that to encourage the person who answered.
- You might say, "I hadn't thought of it that way."
- Sometimes restating the question in different words may help clarify it.
- Recognize every comment. Call the person by name – "Good thought Ryesa, but not exactly what I was asking. Let me try again."

Handling Questions That You Can't Answer
- "I don't know, but I will find out!" Ask if the group has any ideas.
- Don't argue!
- Perhaps ask the group to think about the answer before the next study.

Follow Up the Study

Afterward
- Spend some more time visiting after the study.
- Elicit feedback from participants.
- Be prepared to share the gospel if the opportunity arises.

Between Meetings
- Phone participants.
- Send notes or cards.
- Meet some participants for breakfast, lunch or supper.

Everyone does evangelistic Bible studies similarly but distinctly. The materials above are suggestions. Ask those with experience to share their preferences. When you design your own, make it fit your personality, your goal, and the audience. Some groups are well educated whereas others find it hard to read. The Spirit will direct you, so go for it!

God has determined that prayer and outreach work together (Acts 2-4). The whole process of cultivating quality relationships for Christ must begin with prayer and be sustained by prayer. Colossians 4:2 speaks to this:

> "Devote yourself to prayer, being watchful and thankful. Pray for us, too, that God may open a door for our message, so that we may proclaim the mystery of Christ, for which I am in chains. Pray that I may proclaim it clearly, as I should."

ATTITUDES OF EVANGELISTIC PRAYER (4:2)	AREAS OF EVANGELISTIC PRAYER (4:3-4)
Pray devotedly Ask for the salvation of others as a constant practice.	**Pray for opportunity (3a)** God will give you the chance if you ask Him.
Pray corporately This is written in the plural - we are to pray with others for others.	**Pray for receptivity (3b)** Only the Holy Spirit opens people to the gospel. Ask Him to do so!
Pray alertly Our time is limited and our awareness to opportunity needs to be sharp.	**Pray for tenacity (3c)** Ask God to keep you focused during your difficulties.
Pray thankfully You're part of the process of God giving life to others. What a privilege!	**Pray for clarity (4)** Like Paul, we also want to be guilty of making the gospel clear.
EVANGELISTIC PRAYER	

It's safe to say that we almost all struggle with fear in talking to others about Christ. No one wants to be rejected, disliked, alienated, labeled, or avoided. Fear so grips the average Christian that even when faced with a prime opportunity to speak of Christ, he tends to clam up instead of speak up. Our emotions (fear) can overwhelm our will (faithfulness) in half a heartbeat. That's why so many believers ask, "How can I get rid of my fear of outreach? What can I do to stop being afraid?"

Change Your Focus

Our thinking generates our feelings. Every thought produces a feeling. When you ask, "How can I avoid fear in outreach?" you are asking the wrong question. The need is not to be unafraid, the need is for courage amid your fear. If you focus on your fears, your fears will win out. If you focus on boldness, courage will win. You must change your focus. The appropriate question is not, "How can I get rid of my fear of outreach?" but "How do I get boldness?"

There are two Greek words normally translated "boldness," "courage," "confidence," "open speaking," or "bold." They mean "confidence in public speech" or "freedom to speak openly." Together these words are used 40 times in the New Testament, 26 of them in a context of outreach. What does this reveal?

Whenever these two words occur in the context of outreach, there is *always* a risk of personal harm or injury. Boldness results, therefore, not from the absence of fear or fearful circumstances, but from the conquest of it. Boldness overtakes fear and creates a state of mind from which flows freedom of speech instead of silence. Boldness gives Christians the ability to speak the Gospel with confidence in the face of fear and fearful situations.

After all, isn't that what courage is? Doing what you know you're to do in the face of fear. If you wait for an absence of fear, you will wait forever. Fear flees when you take appropriate action – but only when you take that action. You will get what you aim at; so first, change your focus from fear to boldness. But how?

Boldness Comes When We Have A Heart Full Of Jesus (Matthew 28:1-20)

After His resurrection, our Lord gave us our marching orders. Each gospel has a variation of the Great Commission. Matthew's summary says

Then Jesus came to them and said, "All authority in heaven and on earth has been given to me. Therefore go and make disciples of all nations, baptizing them in the name of the Father and of the Son and of the Holy Spirit, and teaching them to obey everything I have commanded you. And surely I am with you always, to the very end of the age."

Two words, **"then"** and **"therefore"**, connect back to what just happened in verses 1-17. That tie-in helps develop courage, boldness, and confidence in our witness.

Before He gave the Great Commission, Jesus' disciples worshiped Him. If I were to encourage you to worship the Lord, your mind would broadcast a picture of Sunday morning at 11 o'clock. A worship service is not what I have in mind. If you read Matthew 28 carefully, you will find that the disciples' encounters with the resurrected Christ prompted their honest worship, in which some expressed their fears (10) and others their doubts (17). So rather than say, "You need to worship the Lord Jesus," I like to say that you need to get your heart full of who Jesus is.

Outreach wells up from a heart of worship. To genuinely worship Jesus is a transforming experience. When we encounter His transforming presence and power, we will witness spontaneously. Replace your worship service with worship of the Savior – make sure the focus is Him rather than the liturgy. You will be bold when you get a heart full of who Jesus is. Who is he? He is

- **The Faithful One** – He came to the mountain in Galilee as He had promised them (7, 16). Jesus always keeps His word - always - and if you focus on His faithfulness, you will find that He overcomes your fear.

- **The Living One** – He faithfully met His disciples on the mountaintop because He defeated death and lives (16-17). Jesus' resurrection is the heart of the gospel and your guarantee that He and you are victorious. At the same time, because He lives you can discuss with Him your doubts, fears, and worries knowing that He will not condemn you nor reject you but will accept you. In fact, the text states that some doubted . . . *then Jesus came near.* He understands your confusion, doubts, and fears and does not castigate you for them. When you focus on Jesus' victory over death, boldness replaces your fears.

- **THE Authority** - The Father gave Jesus absolute and total authority because of His sinless life, sacrificial death, and powerful resurrection (18-19). Jesus won complete authority over all heavenly, unseen enemies and over all earthly, seen enemies. When fears rise up, remember that Jesus has all authority over you, your words, your listeners, and any seen or unseen enemies. Know that He sent you to represent and to communicate Him with His authority. This is a great confidence builder – He is over all!

- **The Present One** – This is interesting. The great commission starts with Jesus' command to meet Him on the mountaintop (7); there He would be present with the disciples. It ends with His last words, *"Lo, I am with you always, even to the end of the age"* (20). Translations vary, but the words *"surely," "lo,"* and *"behold"* are all different translations of one Greek word that emphasizes the importance of Jesus' presence. His presence is so real that He is persecuted when you are; He feels and shares what you go through (cf. Acts 9:1-5). He wants you to remember that whether you feel His presence or not He is with you - through all the days, good or bad, in all your ways, to the end of the age. Perhaps the greatest boldness builder is to believe that Jesus is present with you.

Fill your heart with Jesus and you will find that your boldness grows. Saturate yourself with the Gospels, the Acts, and Revelation. Rehearse His victory, power, and authority often. Get your heart full of Jesus.

Boldness Comes When We Witness With Others (Acts 2-4; 4:13, 29, 31)

Recall that Jesus called the first disciples to follow Him together – two by two. He chose twelve to be with Him and to preach the kingdom. He sent them out two by two to do just that. On Pentecost Peter stood up with the other eleven apostles to preach. Acts 4:1-22 records Peter's and John's arrests as they witnessed together. Doing outreach together is the norm in Acts (Acts 4:13,29,31).

Through the rest of Acts, Paul traveled and evangelized with teams. The biblical norm in fishing for men is that we link together. Of course, we speak on our own, but the New Testament witness is usually done with others. When you and a friend or two are speaking of Christ, you feel safer and more confident, knowing that "I'm not alone."

You would be wise to complete the Evangelistic Styles survey on page 29 in BMW's *Fostering The Harvest* workbook. Have several of your friends take it with you to determine how you can use each other's strengths and weaknesses to make a good outreach team. This will build everyone's confidence.

With others you're more likely to speak up when the opportunity pops up. Boldness comes from witnessing together.

Boldness Comes When We Ask For Boldness (Acts 4:23-31)

Boldness rarely comes naturally. Even the great apostle Paul experienced fear in outreach. He testified about his ministry in Corinth, "*I was with you in weakness, in fear, and in much trembling*" (1 Corinthians 2:3).

The reason individuals in the New Testament are often said to be bold is that they asked God for boldness and He gave it! Paul wrote, "*We were bold in our God*" (1 Thessalonians 2:1-2). Paul requested boldness from God and asked others to pray with him for boldness (Ephesians 6:19-20).

In Acts 3, Peter and John healed the lame man at the temple gate. Peter used the crowd's amazement to preach the resurrected Christ. Unable to refute the miracle, yet unwilling to believe in Christ, the rulers decided the only alternative was to command Peter and John "*not to speak at all nor teach in the name of Jesus*" (4:18). Dismissed from the presence of the rulers, what did Peter and John do? They returned to the fellowship where they all prayed that God would grant boldness (29), and God did: "*They were all filled with the Holy Spirit, and they spoke the word of God with boldness*" (31).

Witnessing saints pray differently, with urgency. Outreach transforms our upreach. They prayed Psalm 2 about the Gentiles coming revolt against Jesus in the Tribulation. First, they recalled God's control (24), even and especially in persecution. Next, they rested in God's plan, which includes opposition to Christ and the church. Finally, they requested God's power to boldly speak up when the opportunity came up. And God answered! When we jointly pray and preach Jesus, He is there with power. Boldness comes from praying together. Pray for boldness and believe God for it.

Boldness. We all want it and most of us need it. To be bold is to speak up when the opportunity pops up. Where do we get this boldness? Boldness comes from changing your focus, getting a heart full of Jesus, witnessing together, and praying together for boldness.

To lead with neither title, position, nor appointment is a challenge for anyone. Those who attempt to lead an ingrown fellowship into a more outward focused vision and practice may have to lead this way. Thankfully, Scripture and common sense will help us if we must lead in this fashion.

Biblical Truths About Leading Without Position

There are tremendous non-title leadership lessons throughout the records of David's life in 1 Samuel. Chapter 17 is the story of Goliath. David's first leadership assignment was self-appointed; he went after Goliath because the people were too afraid to act. ***Leaders lead because there is some cause worth leading. No one else is taking leadership, and they are willing to risk their personal comfort and reputation to see it through to completion.***

In 1 Samuel 23 David saved a city without any assigned position of leadership. Sure, he had been anointed to be king, but he wasn't yet sworn in to office. He was a king in waiting but rejected by those in power. ***Authentic leaders don't need to have a position to make a difference.*** We will learn more from David later. For now, realize both the reality and necessity of leading with no title. Here are some helpful considerations:

Clarify Your Goal

It can be easy to get sidetracked when leading without support or position. To prevent you from getting off track, know what you want to achieve.

What exactly do you want to accomplish? What is your intended result? What outcome do you want from your leadership? Will it biblically help your church fulfill Christ's purpose? How? Can you do it righteously?

If you can affirm these questions, write down the goal. Keep it before you. Cover it in prayer. Think carefully about strategy to accomplish it. Clarity is critical.

Evaluate the Leadership Atmosphere Where You Are

All organizations operate by shared values, attitudes, and priorities. Many times these are unspoken and unrecognized although they drive the ministry. Quite often the values of established leadership differ from those who influence from below.

After clarifying your objective, evaluate what type of leadership atmosphere pervades your church culture. This tone will affect your leadership activities, progress, time frame, and relationships to a tremendous degree. This means thinking clearly about the leaders over you. As you reflect, DO NOT destructively criticize. DO evaluate constructively.

Is It An Atmosphere Where Control Dominates?
- The leader's ideas win over the team's ideas almost every time.
- The team follows but not too willingly.
- Demands change through fear and guilt, not motivation, vision.
- People are managed but not led, developed nor trusted.
- Team members feel unappreciated and under-utilized.
- The skills and ability of the controlling leader limit the organization.
- Burnout is common.

Is It An Atmosphere Where Influence Dominates?
- The ultimate priority is what's best for the ministry.
- The team develops as relationships and trust grow.
- Willing followers are attracted.
- New leaders are recruited and built.
- Change is promoted through desire, not obligation.
- The organization uses the expanded resources of a team.
- People feel empowered and appreciated.

Now that you have evaluated the climate in your situation, do five things. First, realize that *influence will always trump control* so make up your mind to lead by influence rather than position and control. Secondly, discuss with God whichever culture is primary. Ask Him for wisdom to respond constructively. Third, if it is influence, thank Him and start pursuing your goal while you learn by watching and listening to other leaders. Fourth, if control, look for the easiest and smallest place that you can start to effect change. Fifth, start.

Demonstrate Healthy Influencing Skills (Philippians 2:19-22)

As Paul writes to the Philippians he refers to or implies several leadership-by-influence skills that Timothy displayed as Paul's aide. Give some thought to implementing these:

- Show genuine care for those that you lead (2:19-21).
- Focus on Christ's interests, not yours. Keep the eternal thing the main thing (2:21).
- Demonstrate faithfulness to your superior in the tasks that he assigns you (2:22).
- Relate to your superior with respect – like a son with his father (2:22).
- Give him time to make decisions – be patient (2:22-24).

These approaches will help you earn the affection, trust and respect of those over you even if they may not currently see your viewpoint. Most leaders, however, if responded to in the right way, will begin to see you as more of a helper than a hindrance. Try these Biblical and practical approaches and see if they help you lead without position.

Sometimes when you lead without position, your very presence can create tension. You may do nothing wrong yet find yourself in a tight spot. Sometimes differing values create stress. Personal insecurities and goals can also lead to conflict. How do you respond well should you find yourself in a difficult place as you lead without title?

First Samuel 24 is familiar to us. It records a time when David almost took advantage of an unbelievable opportunity to kill Saul and take the kingdom. It's the story of Saul's trip to the bathroom in David's cave while David cut off the corner of Saul's robe. It shows us.

When Tensions Arise, Don't. . .
- Take advantage of your leader's vulnerability (1-3).
- Listen to those who recommend rebellion (4-5).
- Rebel and then say, "The Lord led me . . ." (5-6).
- Live with a guilty conscience if you do disrespect or demean your boss (5).

When Tensions Arise, Do. . .
- Confront any who give sinful, rebellious advice (6-7).
- Respectfully explain your behaviors and converse with your superior (8-11).
- Wait on the Lord to change people and circumstances (12-15).

Leading from below, or leading up as it is sometimes called, is a strong challenge. You don't want to create division or schisms. You're probably impatient to reach your goal; remember to go slow. Above all, pray, pray, pray. Remember, Christ aims to work in you more than He intends to work through you.

Are we too busy? Oh yeah! Imbalanced? You bet. Apathetic? Probably not. Sure, there are always a few, but it seems that most believers care about the lost; they are just too frenetic, out of round, and not equipped to effectively engage the lost. A prescription for these illnesses addresses two parts: one, the role of the church and two, the role of the believer. We'll start with the church; most believers get their philosophy of life and ministry from church.

Would you say that despite the large number of churches, most have little or no apparent influence in their communities? Some of these churches have departed from sound doctrine and the sufficiency and primacy of Scripture. However, many evangelical, Bible-believing churches fall into this category.

One major factor is the church culture, the mindset of the leaders and members. By nature, people gravitate toward others who share their values. We tend to open up more with those who are like us, people with whom we feel safe.

This may be why most churches (if they grow at all) grow by transfer. They attract people who are already accustomed to that church culture; they know it and are comfortable with how it works. The idea of growing by conversion is something that churches endorse but rarely, if ever, experience.

If you feel that these observations are valid and significant, here are some ideas for you or your church to consider about your church culture and busyness, apathy, or imbalance.

Evaluate Your Church Atmosphere

Find out the truth. It's easy for us to see what we want to see. It's also easy to miss what's really there. As you think about your church, there are three unerring revelators of reality. These three never lie nor misguide.

- First, check the church calendar. What percent of events is outreach oriented?
- Check your budget. What percent is local outreach oriented?
- Listen to announcements. What percent is outreach oriented?

Individuals and groups reveal their true values by their time and money expenditures and by what they talk about. Check those of your church. What is your atmosphere? Inward focused or outward aimed? Find the truth.

Are you about belief or behavior? Do you try to put the cart before the horse? I know it is a cliché, but it is true nonetheless. Sometimes we try to impose our standards of right and wrong on people before we share Christ with them. We often talk more with the lost about behaving than believing. This is one reason people feel judged by believers.

If we are behavior oriented, people may get the impression that if they don't drink, don't smoke, and do show up at church regularly, they are OK. How frightening in light of the radical, life-changing message of grace. Remember, teaching them to obey (behavioral change) is the last part of the Great Commission. Believers need to behave, but the lost need to believe. What message do you export to your community?

Are you for or against? Sometimes churches or groups are more known for what they stand against rather than what they are for. Anytime a church gets a reputation of being against (or even for) something over and above the preeminence of Jesus Christ, there is a major problem based on deeper issues. Nothing, absolutely nothing, should cloud the church's message of the gospel of Jesus Christ or have priority over it. What would a lost person say that your church is about? What would a member say?

Are you about effectiveness or maintenance? In many churches nothing significant has changed in years. Maybe nothing insignificant has changed either. Churches often opt, unintentionally, to just keep things going rather than forging ahead. There is a place for maintenance, but Christ commands the church to be proactive about making disciples, and this starts with evangelism.

When did you last evaluate a ministry program? Can your fellowship state your church mission? What is your evangelism strategy? How do you know if you are succeeding? We cannot afford to assume that attendance is faithfulness. We cannot assume that faithfulness is effectiveness either. We need both, and the latter demands evaluation, change, discomfort, and movement. Let's not settle; let's forge ahead for the gospel. BMW can help you here; they have several proven seminars to help you increase your ministry effectiveness.

Are you about coming or going? As mentioned above, is your ministry system balanced between building up and reaching out? How often does the church program bring participants into contact with the lost? Train them to walk well among the lost? Are you balanced between attending and infiltrating?

Are you proactive in the community? Does your church have a "here we come" outlook rather than a "ya'll come" mentality? In other words, what is your church doing to meet people where they are in the community? Jesus did not just hang around the synagogues and temple waiting for people to come to Him. He pursued people on their turf. Are you?

The first step in helping the church body deal with busyness, apathy, and imbalance is to evaluate the church as a whole, especially the atmosphere. If the atmosphere needs clearing, the following may help.

If you breathe nitrogen for a few minutes, we will shortly attend your funeral. Erupting volcanoes take lives through the change in atmospheric content caused by spewed ash, sulfur, etc. The pulverized concrete, paper, plastic and metal in the air harmed hundreds who were around the Twin Towers on 9/11. Atmosphere is critical to health.

Many of our churches need to create an atmosphere where we breathe outreach as a way of life. This will replace busyness, imbalance, and just about wipe out apathy. So how can we clean our corporate air if we need to? Following are suggestions to help build a culture that embraces outreach as a lifestyle. I have tested and proven these principles for over thirty years.

The Church Can Create A Lifestyle Outreach Buzz

We do what we think and talk about. Therefore, the leadership needs to think and talk about evangelism both privately and publicly. In time this will filter all the way down to the nursery! Here are some suggestions:

- Pray in corporate meetings, especially Sunday AM, about fruitful outreach.
- Do at least one pulpit series a year on outreach equipping.
- Do at least one SS quarter a year on outreach equipping.
- Have someone, especially the leaders, share one outreach testimony a month.
- Pastor can regularly tell stories about his own evangelistic experiences.
- Appoint no leaders who do not regularly evangelize.
- Show a one- to three-minute video about outreach each month.
- Mention good outreach books from the pulpit and in classes.
- Build new member classes around expecting them to share Christ.
- Celebrate every step forward and help create expectancy.
- Include in each sermon, somewhere toward the end, how application of its truth will impact the body's outreach to the community.
- Have everyone list one lost person in the community that they want to see Christ save. Then, let them exchange those names with another member and pray for each other's list by name at least once a week. This will get them talking about lost people and build in a little fellowship and accountability.
- Teach the Great Commission for what it says – disciple as we go. Our folks often make a mental divide between evangelism and missions. Actually, that's our division. Scripture just sees disciple-making everywhere. Help people grasp that the Great Commission begins in their backyard and in their office.
- Be positive, positive, positive; God is for you and outreach is Christ's mission!

The Church Can Equip For Lifestyle Outreach

- Pray about it, pray about it, pray about it, pray about it, pray about it.
- Pastor and leaders must model outreach and take members along.
- Ask the body what they want to know about outreach and then equip them.
- Focus on equipping – HOW & HANDS over teaching WHAT & CONTENT.
- Have one or two classes a year where the gospel is clarified and people practice sharing. These will be age appropriate and cover every age group in the church.
- Have 2 or 3 annual events designed to connect with the lost and/or serve the community.
- Motivate with grace, stories, opportunity, joy and satisfaction. Do NOT use the should-and-ought guilt stuff.
- Applaud faithfulness in mission over faithfulness in attendance.
- Talk about it, talk about it, talk about it, talk about it, talk about it, talk about it.

The Church Can Structure For Lifestyle Outreach

- Proactively budget, calendar, and talk about outreach.
- Comprehensively have each ministry (SS, Worship, Youth, Fellowship, etc.) plan together annually to include outreach.
- Eliminate some calendared events, church meetings, etc. to give your membership more time to be among the lost.
- Know that Sunday is truly the only day that people have discretionary time; structure the ministry so that they are free to be with the lost.
- Play softball in the industrial league rather than the church league.
- Encourage parents to have their kids play soccer in community rather than church leagues.

Use these suggestions as primers to get your creative juices flowing. Genuinely evaluate where you are and how you are as a church.

This is not a paid political advertisement, but if you have read this far, congratulations! You are still interested. Well, boot up and email Biblical Ministries Worldwide at bmwhq@biblicalministries.org. Or, pick up the phone and call BMW at 770.339.3500. BMW has a series of incredible seminars to help your church become more effective. Discuss these proven and powerful opportunities with them; BMW is here to serve you.

If changing priorities and reducing busyness starts with the congregation, what about the individuals who comprise that group? Glad that you asked; keep reading.

Evangelism in modern America isn't what it used to be. Our message hasn't changed, but the environment in which we propagate that message has completely transformed. To be biblically true to our task in this generation, we have to keep some Biblical principles in mind. Here are four:

The Great Commission Is Your Personal Mission

This isn't somebody else's job. It's yours. It is true that the Spirit specifically gifted some to be evangelists and pastors (Ephesians 4:11), but it is also true that the New Testament pattern is that everybody shared the good news regardless of whether they thought themselves specially gifted or not.

The first thing Jesus said to his new disciples was, *"Follow me and I will make you fishers of men."* One thing is for sure: followers are fishers. Jesus spent the first several months with these men showing, sending, and speaking to them about outreach. If we follow Christ, we fish for men.

Remember the woman at the well from John 4? She met the Messiah and proceeded straight into town to tell others about him (John 4:39). And then there's the demon-possessed man, who, after being healed, wanted to stay with Jesus. But Jesus told him to *"go home to your family and tell them how much the Lord has done for you"* (Mark 5:20).

But the one that seals the deal comes from Acts 8:1. The Scripture says that *"all **except the apostles** were scattered throughout Judea and Samaria"* because of the persecution in Jerusalem. Then the Scripture says, *"**Those who had been scattered** preached the word everywhere they went"* (8:4). The leaders of the church were in Jerusalem (the apostles and big name pastors and evangelists) and all those scattered (the regular people like you and me) spread the word.

Get Your Values Straight

Let's face it; most of us *are* too busy to evangelize. Hurried, stressed, overburdened - these words describe us daily. We have no time to reach the lost, and time is what we need. So, before anything else, we need to make time in our schedules to invest in the lost around us. How do we do this?

First, you'll need to cut some of your church activities: don't abandon your church, but ask Christ and yourself if the list of things that you do there is critical. Reduce yourself to one ministry only. Then you'll need to cut some kid stuff: make time for your children first, but ask Christ and yourself if they really need to be involved in sports, dance, piano, art, and band all at the same time year round.

And then there's me stuff and work stuff. The core problem here is selfishness. It may be our drive to climb the corporate ladder or our "need" to play golf every Saturday or watch football all day Sunday. What little discretionary time we have is quickly chewed up by putting self first.

Repent

Shut the door. Turn off the TV. Pause the CD player. Take the battery out of your phone. Shut down your IMac, IPad, IPhone, IPod and any other electronic device. Settle your heart in the quietness. It may take a while; you are used to going hard.

Now spend some time with Christ. Talk to Him about outreach, and be honest. Tell him your fears, concerns and doubts. Ask him your questions. But most of all, let the Spirit examine your heart. What thinking needs to change so that you view life more as your mission? What may need to change in your schedule? What family decisions need to be made?

Sacrifice, it seems, is the fuel in the Great Commission. From its inception, it has exacted a heavy price from those who obey it. Here are some personal sacrifices it may require of you. *[Note: The three paragraphs below are from an undocumented source.]*

- **Relationships you hold dear and enjoy as they are.** As you allow God to identify the lost in your circle of influence, he may burden you to risk a relationship that is important to you, like a close family member, a coworker, or friend at school.

- **Financial welfare in terms of promotions and employment.** The workplace is a ripe field for promoting Christ. As our society stands today, however, evangelizing at work can bring serious consequences. We can lose a promotion or even our job, but how else can we win them if we stay silent and comfortable?

- **Reputation and standing in your circle - the risk of abandonment and loneliness.** We all want to be held in high regard by the people we know. But make no mistake; when you begin to promote Jesus, people will never think of you in the same way.

Discuss these possibilities with the Lord. If you need to change your mind and then your actions, do. He is for you and will respond to your faith and obedience.

Expect God to Work Beyond Your Dreams

It's easy to think no one will listen, that God has moved his work elsewhere, and you're left to fend for yourself. You're willing to do the hard work, but deep inside you don't really believe anything remarkable will happen. That's where you're wrong.

I came to Christ in my twenties from a pagan background. I love lost people and feel like I somewhat understand their lives. I like being with them. A few years back, my heart was dissatisfied. My life was all about believers. I was a pastor and a Bible college instructor. But it frustrated me; when lost persons found out what I did, a curtain seemed to fall. They were polite, but that was it. Relationships with my neighbors were healthy but slow. I was just unsettled, so I began to ask God to bring some lost person into my life. I wanted to share Christ and to lead by example.

One morning the secretary buzzed me to say that the president of a local bank was on line one. I'd never heard of him, so curiosity kicked in, and I picked up. He introduced himself and told me that he had met a woman who knew me through a Business After Hours meeting. (I'd talked with her once at some business affair downtown but could not recall her face.) In their conversation, she told him that I was a good Bible teacher. He then said that he wasn't sure why, but he wanted someone to teach a weekly Bible study to his employees before work. He clarified that he himself did not believe it and would not often come, but he thought it would be good for morale. Would I be willing to teach a 45-minute study each Tuesday morning at the bank at 8 AM? I could teach whatever I wanted as long as it was the Bible.

After I got up off the floor, I passed out again. Actually, I made him repeat it all; maybe I'd finally snapped! Then I said, "Yes" and later that day moved my bank accounts there!

As it turned out, we moved away not too long after. But for over 6 months, we had an evangelistic study with 10-15 persons each Tuesday morning. No one trusted Christ as far as I know; but my last day in town, God put His OK on the experience. I went to the bank to close my accounts. It was the main branch downtown, and the lobby is probably 100 feet across. I walked in, and several of the employees called out my name, waved, and said, "Come see me before you leave."

Some minutes later, I made my way toward the door for the last time. One of the Bible study ladies was behind her desk on the other side of the lobby. She said in a loud voice that everyone heard, "Thanks for the Bible study, Rick. It's given me so much to think about; I'd believe like you if I wasn't a Mormon, but I'm thinking."

All that just because I prayed.

Appendices
PRACTICE FOSTERING THE HARVEST

The following questions and answers are brief but sufficient responses to challenges and concerns that people have about following Christ and embracing Christianity. It would be well for you to memorize one verse for each question and to review the responses several times. Enjoy! *[Note: I have compiled these answers over many years. They are not original with me and are from undocumented sources.]*

Aren't All Religions The Same But Use Different Names For God?

When you look beneath the surface, you'll find out that there are major differences among the religions - even including contradictions about who God is. For example, some forms of Buddhism teach that there is no God; Hinduism teaches that God exists, and that everything is part of Him; Christianity teaches that God exists, but that He is separate from all He has created. These are mutually exclusive definitions. They cannot possibly describe the same God.

Other religions generally view Jesus as being on more or less the same level as other prophets, not as who He claimed to be: God who came to earth as a man (John 1:1, 14; 8:24).

Other religions deny the biblical teaching that Jesus' ultimate mission was to give His life on the cross as a payment for our sins (Matthew 20:28). They also overlook the fact that of all the religions in history with leaders claiming to be from God, Jesus alone backed up His claims by rising from the dead.

In both Old Testament and New Testament days, there were other religions in existence, and the biblical writers clearly viewed them as unacceptable alternatives (Numbers 25:3-5; 1 King 18:16-40; and 1 Corinthians 10:20). For further information about various religions and sects, see **The Kingdom of the Cults**, by Walter Martin; **Cults, World Religions, and the Occult**, by Kenneth Boa; and **Dissonant Voices**, by Harold Netland.

As Long As You're Sincere, Does It Matter What You Believe?

The problem is that sincerely believing something doesn't make it true. You can be sincere, but sincerely wrong. People who get on an airplane that later crashes may be sincere in their beliefs that they would be safe, but their sincerity doesn't change what actually happens. Our beliefs, no matter how deeply held, have no effect on reality.

This is true in all areas of life. Sincerely believing it is safe to cross the road doesn't help you if there's traffic coming. Thinking the speed limit is 65 when it's 45 won't prevent you from getting a ticket for speeding. Strongly holding to your beliefs about God doesn't make them true. Sincerity did not change the facts or the outcome for the people in situations like the mass suicides of the Jim Jones cult in Guyana in the early 1980s or the David Koresh cult in Waco, Texas.

What counts is not the sincerity of our faith, but the **object of our faith**. We need to ask ourselves, "Is what I'm trusting in really trustworthy?" then do our homework to find out whether it is or is not. We need to heed the advice the Bible gives in 1 Thessalonians 5:21: "*Test everything. Hold on to the good.*" For further information read Chapter 1, question 4, in **Give Me an Answer**, by Cliff Knechtle.

If God Loves Us, Why Doesn't He Do Something About All The Evil?

I struggle with this difficult question at times. One thing that has helped me with it, though, is the realization that the evil isn't all out there. There is evil in me and in you, too. If God decided to get rid of all of the evil, He'd have to destroy us as well.

God also created us with the ability to choose. We have the ability to love and follow Him or to reject and turn away from Him. We chose to rebel against Him and to follow our own inclinations. Romans 3:23 explains that we "*all have sinned and fall short of the glory of God,*" and Romans 6:23 adds that "*the wages of sin is death . . . .*" Knowing that we are all part of "the evil" that people say "God should do something about" gives us a new and important perspective.

The Bible does say that God will one day judge all evil. But right now He patiently gives us an opportunity to choose Christ and receive the forgiveness that He offers. He promises to one day not only remove evil but to restore all and to make all things new.

God promises that He will put an end to evil. But He hasn't done so yet. He's waiting, because we matter to Him and He wants more of us to turn to Him. The Bible says in 2 Peter 3:9b, "*He is patient with you, not wanting anyone to perish, but everyone to come to repentance.*" But we must not take His patience for granted; there's no way of knowing how long we'll have to receive His mercy and forgiveness.

Contrary to what we might first think, the existence of evil should lead us toward belief in God, not away from it. If there were no God, then there would be no standard of right and wrong. We would have no way to recognize the differences between good and evil.

Finally, God suffered the ultimate evil when Christ became sin. It's not academic with God. Evil and suffering are personal. He knows how it feels and what it can do. For further information read the section on "Questions about Evil" in **When Skeptics Ask**, by Norman Geisler; and **The Problem of Pain**, by C. S. Lewis.

Why Doesn't God Help Innocent People Who Suffer, Like Little Children?

We cannot claim to understand all the whys of what happens, but we can affirm that Christ is there to meet us in our pain. Avoid giving simplistic answers to this very difficult question. Many times people raise it out of their own pain more than out of a desire to hear a rational answer. Often their need is for personal care, not proper answers. You might respond with, "That's a huge question. Have you suffered greatly?"

After we listen and empathize, we can also tell them that God understands suffering personally. He endured awful and unjust pain when His Son suffered. God knows how we feel. To God, the suffering caused by evil is not some abstract idea. God came to earth as a man for the purpose of suffering evil by taking our evil and its penalty on His back when he died on the cross. In 1 Peter 2:24 it says, "*He himself bore our sins in His body on the tree, so that we might die to sins and live for righteousness; by His wounds you have been healed.*" The truth is, Christ suffered under evil in ways that none of us ever will.

You can also point out that most of the evil in the world stems from people hurting other people! He could stop us from harming each other, but He'd have to limit or take away our freedom of choice to do it. Needless to say, most people are not interested in having God limit their independence. For His own reasons, God lets us choose which way to go in the hope that many of us will turn from our self-centeredness to follow Him.

Finally, the Bible is realistic about the condition of the world we live in. In an age where so many religions and philosophies are trying to convince us that things are getting better and better, or that evil isn't real, it's heartening to see how realistic the Bible is about the world around us. Just watch the six o'clock news or look at some of the struggles in your own life, and you'll see how accurate Jesus was when He said in John 16:33, "*In this world you will have trouble. But take heart! I have overcome the world.*" Suffering certainly is a problem, but we see Christianity is credible in that it accurately and honestly portrays that problem. But remember, answers don't bring comfort. A gentle arm around the shoulder is much more effective. For further information read Chapter 10 in **Know Why You Believe**, by Paul Little; and **When God Doesn't Make Sense**, by James Dobson.

How Do You Know That God Exists?

I don't know it and can't prove it, but here are some excellent reasons for why I believe it. Science points to the order in the universe and that earth is precisely suited for human life. One of many examples of this is that even the slightest variation in the tilt of the earth's axis would result in our either freezing or burning up.

We see order in the human body. We know that something as complex as a wristwatch had to have been made by an intelligent designer. But the hand that wears the watch is far more complex than the watch is. An intelligent designer must certainly have made it. Think how much more this must be true of the whole human body!

Other arguments can be given, such as God being the only adequate cause for the existence of the universe (otherwise it was either eternal itself or it produced itself out of nothing) and God being the only adequate source of morality among humans (otherwise nothing is really right or wrong - we are only left with preferences). But most people don't need to be overwhelmed with reasons as much as to know that you have thought through this important question and accept God's existence for reason, not on blind faith. For further information read **Can A Man Live Without God?** by Ravi Zacharias and **Darwin On Trial** by Phillip E. Johnson.

Who Are You To Say That You're Right And Everyone Else Is Wrong?

First, remember that the argument is not really with us; it was Jesus Himself who said boldly in John 14:6, "*I am the way and the truth and the life. No one comes to the Father except through me.*"

Wisdom often leads us to follow a certain course of action over the many other options. For example, when our family doctor prescribes a medication to help us get well, it's not narrow minded to accept their advice, even though we know there are psychic healers and tribal witch-doctors who would urge a different approach. The question is who has credentials we can trust?

Finally, it's not narrow minded if you've looked into it and found that Christianity proves itself trustworthy in ways that other religions and viewpoints do not.

When someone condemns our views for being exclusive, that person is, at that very moment, doing the very thing they are condemning by excluding our beliefs. The important question is whether or not we have good reason to accept our position over all of the other options.

Avoid confusing truth and tolerance - they are two very different things. We should hold strongly to what we believe and communicate it clearly but also support the rights of others to disagree with our viewpoint. For further information read Chapter two in **Reason to Believe**, by R. C. Sproul.

What Makes You So Confident That The Bible Is True?

Here, you might offer a book that will answer your friends' questions about the Bible. This is wise when we don't have a succinct answer at our fingertips or when it doesn't seem like an ideal time and place to go into it. It's okay to defer to reliable sources of information, such as a credible book or teacher. Or, if it seems preferable, tell them that you would like to study the question and talk with them more about it in a few days. Your friends are more concerned about getting a good answer than an instant one.

Also, encourage your friends to read the Bible for themselves to see if God might speak to them through it. One of the most effective ways to help others see that the Bible really is God's word is to get them to read it for themselves. It will help them get rid of their stereotypes concerning its contents, show them how relevant its teachings are, provide an environment in which the Holy Spirit can powerfully work to convict them of their need, and point them toward the truth. Generally, it is a good idea to direct them to the New Testament as a place to start reading. Romans is great for a logical person, while John is marvelous for one who enjoys stories.

If there really is a God like the one the Bible describes, then it would be no problem for Him to guide many different writers in different lands and different times to faithfully record His message. That, in fact, is what the Bible claims He did (2 Peter 1:20-21). An examination of the Bible itself bears this out. The consistency of the message from Genesis through Revelation is astonishing. Most so called contradictions are easily explained with a little study and reflection. Further, the fact that there are superficial differences in the way the biblical eyewitnesses described what they saw is just further evidence that their testimonies are authentic.

Jesus Himself endorsed the Bible as the Word of God (Matthew 15:6). Repeatedly, He appealed to its authority by saying, "*it is written.*" In John 10:35 He said, "*Scripture cannot be broken.*" Since most people say that Jesus was at least a good teacher, we ought to urge them to take seriously what He taught concerning the Bible.

History, geography, archaeology, and science strongly support the reliability of the Bible. No other book – religious or secular - enjoys this kind of broad support. Study in these areas has changed the minds of many skeptics who doubted the validity of Christianity.

What Evidence Backs Up The Claims Of Christianity?

There were detailed prophecies written about Jesus hundreds of years before he was born. No ordinary person could fulfill these, but He fulfilled every one of them.

Examples include Isaiah 53, which predicted almost 800 years prior to the events that the Messiah would be rejected, that He would "*carry our sorrows,*" that He would pay for our sins (it says in verse 5 that He would be "*pierced for our transgressions*"; this was hundreds of years before crucifixion had been invented as a method of executing criminals), and that he would come back to life (verse 11). Other key passages include Psalm 22 which predicts details of Jesus' crucifixion, including that His hands and His feet would be pierced (verse 16), and Micah 5:2 which announced that He would be born in Bethlehem.

There's other evidence, like His miracles and His teachings. He not only taught the highest moral standards; He also lived them. He predicted that He would come back to life after He died on the cross, and He did it!

Jesus' actions were so completely consistent with His high moral teachings that when His opponents wanted to accuse Him of wrongdoing, they had to make up things that weren't true. For example, at the trial before they crucified Jesus, they relied heavily on false accusations to build their case against Him (Mark 14:56-59). Earlier, He even challenged them by saying, "*Can any of you prove me guilty of sin?*" (John 8:46). His point was clear: they could not do so, nor has anyone else been able to throughout history. This is in stark contrast to every other person who has ever lived.

Also, Jesus' resurrection is supported by the fact that His body vanished from His carefully guarded tomb. The Jewish and Roman leaders would have quickly squelched the talk of a risen Messiah if they had been able to point to His crucified body and reassure the people that He was still dead. But they couldn't because He had risen, and there was no body to be found! For further information read **More Than A Carpenter,** by Josh McDowell; **Know Why You Believe,** by Paul Little; and **Reasonable Faith,** by William Lane Craig (Source unknown).

Let Me Illustrate

Here are some simple and effective illustrations that can be applied readily. Since the illustrations are verbal, they can be used in person or over the phone. Stories hit with emotion as well as truth. Read, learn, and employ! *[Note: I have compiled these illustrations over many years. They are not original with me and are from undocumented sources.]*

Baseball

For those with misplaced confidence in religion, especially if the person is a sports fan.

Earning our way into God's favor would be like a baseball player trying to get into an imaginary All Universe Player's Association that requires a minimum twenty-year career batting average of 1000, with no errors. God's standard is like that, requiring us to always do everything God wants and never step outside the boundaries of His commands. Thankfully, that is exactly what Christ, our substitute ("designated hitter"), did for us, followed by dying to pay the full price for our shortcomings.

Airplane

For one who needs to understand that, beyond a right knowledge of the facts, faith is required.

We are often like the woman who wanted to fly to another city. She studied all about aviation, discovered which airline had the safest record, went to the airport, found the right flight, checked over the airplane, and even interviewed the pilot, only to stand on the runway and watch the plane takeoff without her.

Many people know all about the Bible, the Gospel of Christ, and the forgiveness and new life available for the asking. But, they never "get on board" by actually trusting what Christ has done for them.

School

For those who compare themselves to others and believe that, because they think they are morally above average, they are okay. This illustration works especially well with students.

Many people assume that God is like their teachers in school who grade on a curve. However, the Bible tells us that is a false hope. God is completely just and therefore must judge all sin, even "average" sin.

The good news is that, while God does not grade on a curve, he did something even better. He took the test in our place, and He got a perfect score! Jesus Christ did that by living a perfect life in our place, then dying to pay the penalty for our sins. His resurrection proves his perfection. Why not trust Him to "apply His perfect score to your grade book"?

Swimming Across The Ocean

For anyone who struggles with self-righteousness, thinking their goodness will somehow get them to God. This illustration is simple and clear.

Suppose we decided to swim across the ocean entirely unassisted. You might make it farther than I, and an Olympic Gold Medal swimmer would make it farther than either of us. The fact is that nobody can do it. That's the way it is with trying to live up to God's standard. We all fall short (Romans 3:23). We all need help from God to make it, and Christ is that help.

The Judge

For expanding a person's view of who God is and what He did for us.

There is a story of a young person convicted of a crime. The judge, being a good judge, could not just let the lawbreaker off. The penalty the law demanded was imposed - a fine of $10,000.

The fine was totally beyond the young person's ability to pay. But then the judge did an unusual thing. Taking off his judicial robe, the judge came around in front of the bench and paid the fine. The judge did this because the criminal was the judge's child. The penalty had to be paid, but the judge paid it because He loved his son.

You would have to agree that it would not make very much sense for the child to refuse to allow the father to pay the penalty and to insist on going to jail. God is a good judge as well as a loving father. As a judge, He sees our sin and says, "You have sinned against me, the penalty is death, but I will save you and will pay the penalty myself." Then, as a father, He took off His heavenly robe, stepped over to our side of the bench, and paid for our sins by Christ's death on the cross! (Adapted from **More Than a Carpenter**, pages 114-115, by Josh McDowell, 1997)

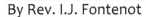

Help Witnessing To Roman Catholics

By Rev. I.J. Fontenot

Witnessing to Roman Catholics is different from other groups. We truly need to grasp their church culture and understand the Roman Catholic religion. How? Spend time with Catholics and ask them various questions about their faith. Second, read the Catechism. Realize that the majority of Roman Catholics don't understand their own religion; they only do as they're told!

Introduction

Roman Catholics believe that they are Christians in a right relationship with God. Many of them are very righteous and very lovely people and often are the finest neighbors and citizens in our communities. In contrast to the above facts, their beliefs and religious practices include many things that are in complete contradiction and conflict to the teaching of the Bible. Multitudes of them who have come into our Bible-believing churches testify that they did not have a personal relationship with Christ until they recognized the error of Catholicism and were taught the truth by an evangelical believer.

The best New Testament parallel to the situation of the Roman Catholic today was the devoutly religious Jew. He believed in God. He believed that the Bible was the Word of God. He worshipped regularly; yet he rejected Christ as personal Savior.

Why did the Jews reject Christ? (Mark 7:1-13)
- They changed their *authority* for faith and morals from the Word of God to tradition or from the Bible to the hierarchy (vs. 5, 9).
- They changed the *meaning* of Scripture (vs. 10-13).
- They changed *responsibility* for personal religious decisions from the individual to the priest (John 9:22).

What is the main difference between Roman Catholicism and Evangelical Christianity?
Their authority for faith and morals is the teaching of the church, not the Bible. They claim that since Christ established the Roman Catholic Church, and gave the successors of the apostles (the popes, bishops, and priests) the ability to interpret and to teach Scripture; individual people must follow church teaching.

It is to be understood that while the New Testaments of the Catholic and Protestant Bibles are just alike, the Old Testaments are different. Our Old Testament contains 39 books. In the Catholic version, in addition to our 39, they have added seven more books and have made additions to Esther and Daniel. They added as books Judith, Tobith, Wisdom, Ecclessiasticus, Baruch, the Epistle of Jeremy, and I and II Maccabees. There is an addition to Esther. The additions to Daniel are Song of the Three Children, Story of Susanna, and Bel and the Dragon. These writing have been called Apocrypha Books. The term means "forged authorship or contents heretical." The reason they are not included in our Bible is because they are not inspired writings. No one counted them to be inspired writings, not even the Catholic Church, until they declared them inspired at the Council of Trent in 1546.

The Hebrew Bible excluded the apocryphal books, and this was the version that the Lord Jesus preached from and called the Word of God - the Holy Scriptures. He referred to most of the books of the Hebrew Scriptures but never once to an apocryphal book. This was the same version used by the apostles, and they counted it to be the Word of God. To our Lord and his apostles, the apocryphal books were not inspired. Likewise, the early Christian scholars, expressing the attitude of the early church, considered them uninspired books.

Jerome, a Christian scholar of the 4th century, translated the Bible into the Latin language. This version was called the Latin Vulgate and was the Roman Catholic Bible through the history of that church. Jerome translated only those 39 books of the Old Testament that we have in our Bible. He said, "Anything outside of these must be placed within the Apocrypha." (Jerome is claimed as a great scholar of the Roman Catholic Church. That is why we quote him here.)

Other early Christian writers (claimed by the Roman Catholic Church to be Catholics) included the same books that Jerome did in their writings, rejecting the apocryphal books because they were not inspired writings. Among them were Tertullian of North Africa, Hilary of France, and Rufimus of Italy. Augustine distinguished between the inspired writings and the uninspired and called the Apocrypha uninspired. Pope Clement VII (1378-1394), in the dedication of his Commentary on Scripture wrote, "The whole Latin church is indebted to St. Jerome for distinguishing the Canonical (inspired) from the non-Canonical (non-inspired) books, since he has freed us from them."

DIALECTICAL TERMINOLOGY		
ROMAN CATHOLIC	**SUBJECT**	**EVANGELICAL**
Baptism	**Born again**	Miracle - believe Once
By faith and works	**Justification**	By faith in Christ
Weekly communion	**Receive Christ**	When we believe
Establish the Sacraments	**Why Christ died**	Vicarious atonement
Merited favor	**Saved by grace**	Unmerited favor
Son of Mary	**Divinity of Christ**	Son of God
Mother of God	**Mary**	Mother of Jesus
After all penance is paid	**Forgiveness of sins**	Moment of salvation
Believing the Church says	**Faith**	Believing the Bible says

The root produces the fruit. To destroy the fruit, one must cut the root! Church authority must give way to biblical authority!

Evangelism In Roman Catholic Cultures

(The psychological characteristics of Roman Catholicism in view of church theology.)

Let's compare the mental attitudes of the Roman Catholics and Evangelicals toward religious things.

The Evangelical Mind: Birth of A Baby
- A blessing from God and a responsibility from God.
- Brought to a nursery for care while parents attend services. Some parents have a dedication service for the child. As soon as he can learn, he is moved into a teaching nursery where he is taught the Bible in some form.
- His total life from birth till he dies, everything he learns spiritually or socially is based upon what the Bible says.
- Believes the Bible to be inspired and preserved; it is the only basis for faith and morals.
- Basis of total culture is the Bible and its authority.

Life's most important decision, the plan of salvation, is known from childhood. More important than life itself is salvation. Even though they may reject Christ in childhood or youth, realization of the need is always present.

Confrontation Evangelism techniques are based upon the above realities and assumptions. Evangelicals understand that commitment can come at anytime in life. The basis for such an experience at any time in life is based upon the cultural as well as religious position of respecting the final authority of the Bible.

The Catholic Mind: The Birth of A Baby

- Christened as a Catholic as soon as possible. This makes it a Christian with the life of God or grace. His total life he is taught that he has the possibility of going to heaven some day if he always obeys the laws of the Roman Catholic Church.

- The church will always authoritatively give him what is proper in faith and practice. The official spokesman is the priest. The Bible is valuable in such things but is the first part of a body of tradition given (he believes) by God for faith and practice. The basis of their total culture is the church and its teaching authority.

- Life's most important function is to always obey the Catholic Church. To question its teachings borders on being a serious sin. They are to avoid being a part of any other church.

Confrontation Evangelism techniques confuse and bewilder him. He assumes such methods to be an attack upon his most priceless heritage, his Catholic religion.

The Roman Catholic and Evangelical have two different systems of mental activity:

The Evangelical

He has an objective mental set for solving and determining questions concerning faith and practice. He has a safe standard, the Bible, that makes it possible for him to objectively make judgments relative to any moral or religious issue. This gives him self-confidence in his right to trust the Holy Spirit to guide him in the process of moral determination. It gives him personal conviction in his conclusions and equips him to personally explain and defend his conclusions and judgments.

The Roman Catholic

He has a subjective mental set for responding to questions concerning faith and practice. He believes he is incapable of determining issues of faith and practice because that is the role of his church. The church has already determined what his faith and practice should always be. If he finds an area in which he is not sure, he must find an official of that church to tell him what is correct. Therefore, he generally will not engage in the kinds of discussions persons accustomed to confrontation evangelism techniques usually try to get him involved in.

Conclusions

Roman Catholic minds are completely conditioned in the above manner. Ability to quote dogma and teaching is not necessary for loyalty to the church. It is engraved in their minds, conscience and culture. Therefore, the basic difference between Roman Catholicism and Evangelical Christianity is in their attitude toward authority.

This leaves the Evangelical with an objective thinking process and the Catholic with a subjective thinking process. This difference in the thinking process is the key to designing effective evangelistic techniques for working with them.

An effective technique must be designed to fit the thinking process and mindset of the Roman Catholic. That process can be done through evangelistic Bible studies. This will involve a discipline of learning to think in a different manner by the Christian worker.

The Catholic who believes will experience some trauma. He must change a lifelong thinking system which is not an easy task. Peter probably experienced a similar trauma when he had to change his life-long thinking system relative to the Gentiles in Acts 10. The difficulty of such a change is seen by the fact that he was still struggling with it many years later when he visited the Gentile churches (Galatians 2).

Evangelistic Relationships With Roman Catholics

You must love him and create a relationship with him in the normal things of life. You must avoid any confrontation with him about his religion at first. You cannot influence him until he likes your influence.

Begin to pray that God will cause something to happen in his life that will cause him to speak to you in a way that you can begin to plant seeds of truth in his mind. Show how the Word of God speaks to his problem or need. Then move from such an experience to saying, "May I show you why I like to read the Scriptures often?"

The beginning dialogue: Thought Starters
- Did you know that St. Peter's description of the end of the world sounds like an atomic explosion? (2 Peter 3:10-13)
- Do you know why the Jews and the Arabs are always fighting? (Genesis 16, 21 - story of Isaac and Ishmael)
- Did you know the Bible describes how things will be in the world toward the end of time? (2 Timothy 3:1-5)

Application

That is the reason I like to read the Scriptures often. They are more up to date than the newspapers. Could I show you why I think it is important to read the Scriptures often? Turn to John 12:46-50. Ask questions in this manner to show that God gave us the New Testament in order to

- Establish the authority of the Word of God
- Know the right information about the person and work of Christ.

As occasion arises, we can explain the true meaning of Biblical terminology. This can be done at the same time we are establishing the authority of Scripture. Encourage them to read the Scriptures. As they see scriptures condemning Catholic dogma, don't use your own words to condemn it, but turn to Scripture passages. Let them read them and draw their own conclusions. Whatever you say, simply point out, "This is what the Bible says."

Explain how to believe in Christ but don't put any pressure on them to do so. The Holy Spirit will do that. Once they understand by the work of the Holy Spirit and they believe, you will know it, and at that point you will do about the same thing in discipling that you would do with anyone else.

Signs of Accepting Biblical Authority

They will begin to find scriptures that condemn Roman Catholic teaching. They will begin to tell other Roman Catholics what they have found in the Scriptures. Lead them to other scriptures that reinforce what they have found.

When this begins to happen, you can then begin to give the proper meaning of Scripture to destroy their dialectical terminology. In fact, you can begin to explain the plan of salvation by having them read the text. This will also get them to see that they are responsible to make their own spiritual decision.

When you have gotten the Roman Catholic to read the Bible in confidence as his final spiritual authority, you have accomplished the main work in leading him to Christ. The Scriptures become a precious new gold mine of truth that he never knew existed and you can lead him to the plan of salvation easily.

Some will accept the Lord, and some will reject Him. We are only God's instruments to show them, but we can be faithful in that work.

The next pages are four evangelistic Bible study lessons from the gospel of John. These are what we give the participants. To use them, the teacher will need to prepare to explain very briefly cultural/historical backgrounds and perhaps a concise interpretation of key terms such as the 'Word' or 'Pharisee'. The goals of these studies are:

- Teach observation of the text
- Build confidence in Scripture
- Expose participants to the living Word
- Plant the gospel seed
- Bring to salvation
- Have something that participants can take home and review

The samples are:

- The Word   John 1:1-18
- What's In A Name   John 1:29-51
- Nic At Nite   John 3:1-21
- Thirsty   John 4:1-42

The Word
John 1:1-18

Read chapter 1:1-18 on page 1143 and answer the questions as best you can. No problem if you get stuck – we'll all discuss them in a few minutes. Have fun!

1.   What is a word? What does it do?

2.   What is unique about the Word in verse 1?

3.   What did the Word do in verse 14?

4.   What is the Word's name in verse 18?

5.   What did the Word communicate in verse 18? How?

What's In A Name?
John 1:29-51

Read chapter 1:29-51 on page 1143 and answer the questions as best you can. No problem if you get stuck – we'll all discuss them in a few minutes. Have fun!

1. Who did John the Baptist say that Jesus is? What did he say that Jesus does?

2. What did the two disciples call Jesus?

3. What did Andrew call Jesus?

4. What did Phillip call Jesus? Why?

5. What did Nathanael call Jesus? Why?

6. What did Jesus call himself?

7. Summarize in your own words who Jesus seems to be.

Nic At Nite
John 3:1-21

Read chapter 3:1-21 on page 1145 and answer the questions as best you can. No problem if you get stuck – we'll all discuss them in a few minutes. Have fun!

1. Why do you suppose that Nicodemus came at night? (1-2)

2. What two things did Jesus say that no one can do without being born again? (3-5)

3. What do you think 'born of flesh' means? 'Born of Spirit?' (5-8)

4. What prompted God to send Jesus? (9-17)

5. How can you have eternal life? What happens to those who do not believe Jesus? (16-18)

Thirsty?
John 4:1-42

Read chapter 4:1-42 on page 1146 and answer the questions as best you can. No problem if you get stuck – we'll all discuss them in a few minutes. Have fun!

1. What does it tell you about Jesus that he was tired and thirsty? That he spoke to a Samaritan woman? (1-7)

2. What do you suppose the woman looked like? Why? (16-18)

3. What type of thirst was Jesus referring to in verses 10-14? What will quench that thirst?

4. How did the woman and her townspeople respond to Jesus? (27-30; 39-42)

The following is taken from the Net. I do not recommend nor endorse any part of the article. It is simply a resource.

The Top 10 Resources for Digital Evangelism Month
May 9, 2011 | Written by Stephanie Harrison

In case you haven't heard, this month is Digital Evangelism Month, and this coming Sunday, May 15th, is specifically Internet Evangelism Day. In light of this, I have created a list in no particular order of the top ten resources we can use during the month to help us reach those in our online spheres of influence.

For a little over a year, I have been involved with EvanTell's social media by managing this blog, our Facebook page, Twitter account, etc. Because we are focused on evangelism, every time I see something online about internet evangelism I'm immediately interested. The resources in this list are ones that have provided the most value to me over the last year and make me want to come back for more.

1. Internet Evangelism Day (IE Day) – *IE Day*'s site includes pages on using mobile phones for evangelism, creating 'outsider-friendly' church websites and introductory videos, social networking, how to blog or build a website, and much else.

2. Digital Evangelism Issues – This is the official blog for the *IE Day* site. I enjoy this blog because it not only gives you digital outreach ideas, but it also tells you what the trends are for the web, mobile phone, video clip, social networking, and more.

3. Sticky Jesus – This site discusses how to live "sticky" online, and the blog posts are consistently a good length for readers. They even have a really good post giving tips for Digital Outreach Month here.

4. YesHeIs.com – This site provides great videos to link to your Facebook status updates, Tweets, or other social media channels that connect your interests to your faith. It helps you share your faith online by helping you link Jesus into everyday life. All the videos are well done and have a really compelling message.

5. Christian Web Trends – I use this site as a resource when I want to know about the news and trends in communications technology and how that impacts Christian organizations. Last year they did a whole blog series on "20 Ways to Share Your Faith Online" found here.

6. Global Short Film Network – This site provides short videos you can download which have underlying Biblical themes. Many of the videos are free if you want to use them on your mobile device or online, but if you would like to purchase them they come with discussion questions you can use to help you start conversations that center around Christ.

7. Probe Ministries – This site provides online articles that can help you dialogue about controversial topics today such as _Terrorism in America_, _Gay Teen Suicide_, and _Abortion_. You could also link these articles to your Facebook or twitter statuses for others to read.

8. GreatCommission2020.com – Need some inspiration for online outreach? View this site's world map with people visiting in real time sites set up to reach unbelievers searching for spiritual topics.

9. Global Media Outreach – This organization utilizes the Internet to help people learn about the Good News of Christ. If you're interested in digital outreach, you can become an Online Missionary who responds to people from all around the world who have requested follow up from one of their sites.

10. GordonMarcy.com – On his personal blog, Gordon Marcy writes about how the Internet and emerging technologies are affecting the way evangelism, discipleship, and building the church are done. I think he's very good at providing excellent content on this subject.

12518182R00031

Made in the USA
Charleston, SC
10 May 2012